OUR FAMILIES

by Stacey Zable

My name is Tess. This is my family.
I live with my mom, dad,
big brother, and little sister.

My dad helps my brother and me get ready for school in the mornings. He walks us to school every day.

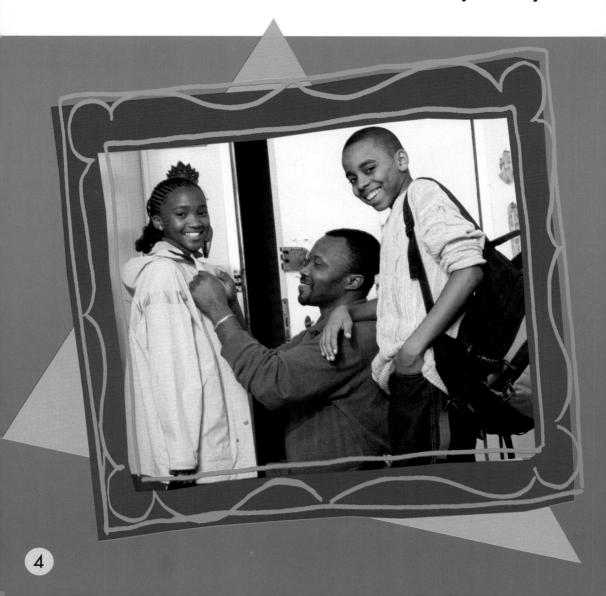

When we come home, Mom gives us a snack. Then Dad helps me with my homework.

My name is Nate.
I live with my dad.
We have a lot of fun together!

This is my dad.
His name is John.

Jane is my baby-sitter. She stays with me until my dad comes home from work.

Sometimes Jane helps me
with my homework. Then we
make dinner together.

My mom does not live with my dad and me. She lives in a different town. I stay with her every weekend.

I like staying with my mom on the weekends. Sometimes I help her do work around the house. ▶

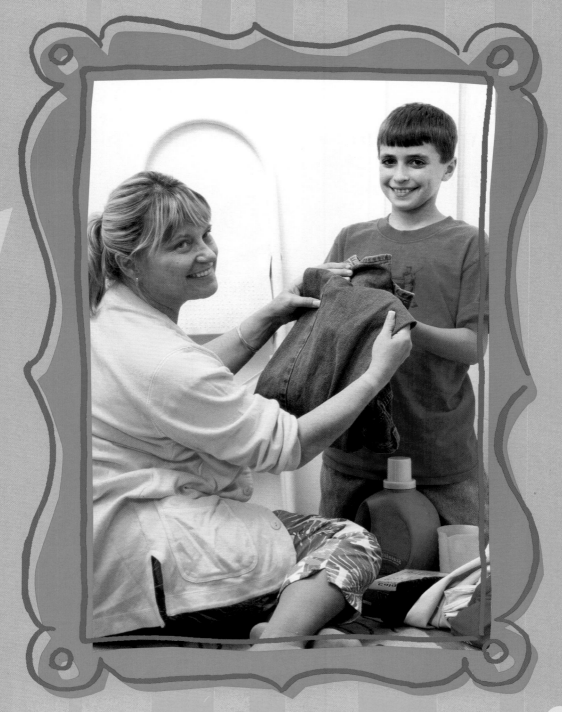

My name is Ann. This is my family. My grandma and grandpa live with my mom, dad, brother, sister, and me.

I am happy that I see *my grandma* and grandpa every day.

My mom and dad work together.

Mom and Dad own
a grocery store.

Grandpa and Grandma stay home with my brother, my sister, and me when my parents are at work.

Sometimes my grandma and grandpa let us play games when we come home from school.

When my parents come home,
we all have dinner together.
I have fun with my family.